Date: 11/5/21

J 323.1196 MAR
Markovics, Joyce L.,
2020 Black Lives Matter
marches /

PROTEST!
March for CHANGE

2020
BLACK LIVES
MATTER MARCHES

by Joyce Markovics

CHERRY LAKE PRESS

Published in the United States of America by Cherry Lake Publishing Group
Ann Arbor, Michigan
www.cherrylakepublishing.com

Reading Adviser: Marla Conn, MS Ed., Literacy specialist, Read-Ability, Inc.
Content Adviser: Emilye Crosby, PhD
Book Designer: Ed Morgan

Photo Credits: © Sue Nilsson/Shutterstock, cover and title page; Wikimedia Commons, 4–5; © Tverdokhlib/Shutterstock, 5 bottom; © Julian Leshay/Shutterstock, 6–7; Wikimedia Commons, 8; Courtesy of Library of Congress, 9; © ESB Professional/Shutterstock, 10 top; © Monkey Business Images/Shutterstock, 10 bottom; © Skyward Kick Productions/Shutterstock, 11; © Ira Bostic /Shutterstock, 11; © Associated Press, 13; © Rena Schild/Shutterstock, 14 left; © a katz/Shutterstock, 14 right; Wikimedia Commons, 15; Wikimedia Commons, 16; Wikimedia Commons, 17; © hkalkan/Shutterstock, 18; © Michal Urbanek/Shutterstock, 19; © Eli Wilson/Shutterstock, 20–21.

Cherry Lake Press is an imprint of Cherry Lake Publishing Group.

Library of Congress Cataloging-in-Publication Data

Names: Markovics, Joyce L., author.
Title: 2020 Black Lives Matter marches / by Joyce Markovics.
Description: Ann Arbor, Michigan : Cherry Lake Publishing, [2021] | Series:
  Protest! March for change | Includes bibliographical references and
  index. | Audience: Grades 2-3
Identifiers: LCCN 2020040924 (print) | LCCN 2020040925 (ebook) | ISBN
  9781534186354 (hardcover) | ISBN 9781534186439 (paperback) | ISBN
  9781534186514 (pdf) | ISBN 9781534186590 (ebook)
Subjects: LCSH: Black lives matter movement—Juvenile literature. | African
  Americans—Violence against—Juvenile literature. | Racial profiling in
  law enforcement—United States—Juvenile literature. | Police
  brutality—United States—Juvenile literature. | Floyd, George,
  1973-2020—Juvenile literature. | Civil rights movements—United
  States—History—21st century—Juvenile literature. | African
  Americans—Social conditions—21st century—Juvenile literature. |
  United States—Race relations—History—21st century—Juvenile
  literature. | Racism—United States—History—21st century—Juvenile
  literature.
Classification: LCC E185.615 .M293 2021 (print) | LCC E185.615 (ebook) |
  DDC 323.1196/073—dc23
LC record available at https://lccn.loc.gov/2020040924
LC ebook record available at https://lccn.loc.gov/2020040925

Printed in the United States of America
Corporate Graphics

C**O**NTENTS

JUSTICE NOW!

"I can't breathe! I can't breathe!" **protesters** shouted over and over in the spring and summer of 2020. They marched as an army of thousands in 2,000 cities and towns across America. The Black, White, and brown protesters pumped their fists in unity. Their message was clear. Police **brutality** and **racism** must end. The marches were sparked after police choked and killed an unarmed Black man in March 2020. His name was George Floyd.

#Ican't BREATH

George Floyd is one of many Black Americans who have been killed by police.

Many of the protesters held homemade signs. A Black man carried a poster that said "Stop Killing Us." Another sign read "Black Lives Matter" in big, bold letters. Some people held up portraits of Floyd. A lot of protesters were marching for the first time ever.

"I was really, really surprised by the amount of people who turned out and how **diverse** the crowd was," said an Indian woman. A White man said he planned to attend as many marches as he could. "I plan on staying the course as long as it takes to achieve **radical** change."

A group called the Black Lives Matter Global Network inspired many of the protests.

7

BLACK LIVES MATTER

The shooting of George Floyd drew attention to the country's ongoing problem of racism. During the 1960s, Black Americans were not allowed to go to the same schools or hospitals as White people in certain areas. They were denied access to vote and some jobs. If they didn't follow the countless harsh rules set up by White people, they faced severe punishment. Thousands of **activists** and ordinary people fought for equal rights for Black Americans.

"We been waitin' all our lives, and still gettin' killed, still gettin' hung, still gettin' beat to death. Now we're tired waitin'!" said activist Fannie Lou Hamer in the 1960s.

The efforts of **civil rights** leaders brought about new laws that helped protect Black people. But this did not stop **structural racism** throughout the country.

A 1940 photo showing a segregated bus station in North Carolina where Black people were kept apart from White people

Structural racism offers White people advantages that Black Americans cannot get. For example, it's more difficult for Black people to get a quality education, live in safe neighborhoods, access healthcare, and find good jobs. This occurs despite laws that protect them from discrimination.

In the recent past, the U.S. government made it harder for Black people to afford housing. This led to crowded slums.

Black people often struggle to get good healthcare.

As a result of structural racism, Black people are six times more likely than White people to be put in prison. Even more troubling, Black men are more than twice as likely to be shot and killed by police as White men.

Because of racism, Black men are viewed as more dangerous than other people. This can lead to false arrests and killings.

In February 2012, a Black teenager named Trayvon Martin was shot and killed on his way home from a store in Florida. The man who shot Martin thought the 17-year-old looked **suspicious** and dangerous. In his trial, the shooter was found not guilty.

Protesters march for Trayvon Martin.

This news saddened many Americans, including three female activists. For them and others, this decision meant that Martin's life and other Black lives didn't matter. To demand justice, they invented the phrase Black Lives Matter.

Black Lives Matter was started by three women: Alicia Garza, Patrisse Cullors, and Opal Tometi.

Two years later, in 2014, police killed a young, unarmed Black man named Michael Brown in Missouri. The policeman who shot Brown multiple times was not charged with a crime. Thousands marched—and kept marching—to protest the killing. This uprising turned Black Lives Matter into a movement.

"Black Lives Matter" means that Black lives should be just as important as other lives.

Justice for Mike Brown!
Arrest Ofc. Darren Wilson for Murder
Stop Racist Police Terror
ANSWER Coalition • AnswerCoalition.org

I CAN'T BREATH!!!

I CAN'T BREATH!!!

RIP
Bro. Eric Garner

That same year, more Black lives were lost. Eric Garner, a father and grandfather, was choked to death by New York police. Tamir Rice, a Black 12-year-old, was shot by a White cop in Ohio. Brown, Garner, and Rice are three of the dozens of Black people who have died at the hands of police in the past 20 years.

Breonna Taylor's memorial in Louisville, Kentucky, where she was shot

The **victims** of police shootings also include women. Police shot Breonna Taylor eight times in her home in 2020.

THE MARCHES

On May 25, 2020, a policeman in Minneapolis, Minnesota, forced George Floyd to the ground. He knelt on Floyd's neck for almost 9 minutes until Floyd stopped breathing. Before he died, Floyd cried out that he couldn't breathe. Onlookers, one of whom took a video of the **incident**, tried to help him. Yet the police refused to stop hurting Floyd.

George Floyd

The video of Floyd's killing spread around the country. It shocked and angered people. Hundreds of thousands of protesters took to the streets to demand justice for Floyd—and the other victims who came before him.

This is where George Floyd lost his life. Teenager Darnella Frazier recorded his arrest and death on her phone.

The protesters marched for something bigger as well. They wanted to stop violence against Black people. They also wanted to hold police who abuse their power accountable for their actions.

Most of marches were peaceful, but some turned violent. Unfortunately, the violent ones were shown more often in the news.

In addition, the Black Lives Matter marchers focused on the widespread problem of structural racism. They demanded that leaders listen. And they called on everybody in the country to take action to fight racism.

Protest marches are an important part of American history. They helped women earn the right to vote and workers get better pay.

A CALL FOR CHANGE

Soon after the marches began, small changes started happening. In Minneapolis, where George Floyd lost his life, the city started taking steps to rethink and reform the role of the police.

However, ending structural racism is a bigger fight. It involves changes to education, healthcare, housing, and jobs so that Black people have the same advantages as White people. "Protest is not the end of progress, it is the beginning. . . . I believe in us," said the musician Lizzo, urging people to keep up the fight.

Hundreds of different organizations fight for racial justice. These include Dream Defenders, BYP100, and Movement for Black Lives.

TIMELINE

2012

February 26
Trayvon Martin is killed in Sanford, Florida.

2013

July 13
Black Lives Matter is formed by Alicia Garza, Patrisse Cullors, and Opal Tometi.

2014

July 17
Eric Garner is killed by police in Staten Island, New York.

August 9
Michael Brown is killed by police in Ferguson, Missouri.

November 22
Tamir Rice is killed by police in Cleveland, Ohio.

2020

March 13
Breonna Taylor is killed by police in Louisville, Kentucky.

May 25
George Floyd is killed by police in Minneapolis, Minnesota.

May 26
Black Lives Matter protests begin in Minneapolis, Minnesota.

GLOSSARY

accountable (uh-KOUN-tuh-buhl) responsible; having to answer to someone for something you did

activists (AK-tuh-vists) people who join together to fight for a cause

brutality (broo-TAL-ih-tee) the state of being cruel or violent

civil rights (SIV-uhl RITES) the rights everyone should have to freedom and equal treatment under the law, regardless of who they are

discrimination (dis-krim-ih-NAY-shuhn) unfair treatment of others based on differences in such things as skin color, age, or gender

diverse (dih-VURS) having many different types or kinds

incident (IN-sih-duhnt) something that happened

justice (JUHS-tis) the quality of being fair and good

portraits (POR-trits) pictures of a person's face

protesters (PROH-tes-turz) people who gather publicly to show disapproval of something and fight for change

racism (RAY-siz-uhm) a system of beliefs and policies based on the idea that one race is better than another

radical (RAD-ih-kuhl) taking a direction that is very different from what's normal and can lead to big changes

reform (rih-FORM) to change something to improve it

structural racism (STRUHK-chur-uhl RAY-siz-uhm) all the systems in a society—such as laws, policies, and attitudes—that create and maintain inequality for Black people and other people of color

suspicious (suh-SPISH-uhs) giving someone the impression that something about you is wrong

uprising (UHP-rye-zing) a revolt or rebellion

victims (VIK-tuhmz) people who are hurt, injured, or killed by a person or event

violence (VYE-uh-luhns) behavior intended to hurt or kill someone

FIND OUT MORE

Books

Henderson, Leah. *Together We March: 25 Protest Movements That Marched into History*. New York: Atheneum Books, 2021.

Hudson, Wade, and Cheryl Willis Hudson, eds. *We Rise, We Resist, We Raise Our Voices*. New York: Crown Books for Young Readers, 2018.

Kluger, Jeffrey. *Raise Your Voice: 12 Protests That Shaped America*. New York: Philomel Books, 2020.

Websites

Britannica Kids—African American History at a Glance
https://kids.britannica.com/kids/article/African-American-history-at-a-glance/623342

PBS Kids—Arthur on Racism: Talk, Listen, and Act
https://pbskids.org/video/arthur/3045272708

Skokie Public Library—Black Lives Matter: A Reading List for Children & Families
https://skokielibrary.info/lists/520/black-lives-matter-a-reading-list-for-children-families

INDEX

ABOUT THE AUTHOR

Joyce Markovics is a writer and history buff. She loves learning about people and telling their stories. This book is dedicated to Black people who have suffered from racism in the United States and around the world—and to all the people who march for a more just future.